FRAIL UNION

POEMS

FRAIL UNION

POEMS

by
NYLAH LYMAN

Encircle Publications, LLC
Farmington, Maine USA

Frail Union ©2021 Nylah Lyman

Paperback ISBN-13: 978-1-64599-278-3
Kindle ISBN-13: 978-1-64599-279-0

Editor: Cynthia Brackett-Vincent
Book and book cover design: Eddie Vincent/ENC Graphics Services
Cover Image: Shutterstock.com

Sign up for Encircle Publications newsletter and specials
http://eepurl.com/cs8taP

Mail Orders, Author Inquiries:
Encircle Publications
PO Box 187
Farmington, ME USA 04938

Online orders:
encirclepub.com

DEDICATION

to Gwenn

TABLE OF CONTENTS

MAKING A FIELD

for Melissa

White towel flaps in an acidic blue sky,
billowing out from a porch you've never seen.

The cabin you helped build from thick red pines
rots like an old tooth in the encroaching forest,

which you once beat back to the hillside, a hundred acres or more,
with nothing but oxen and scythe.

It's sinking fast now, receding into the soft gumline
of discarded leaves and moss.

I believe that some things had to go:
gated cemeteries in the woods

full of the graves of soldiers and unnamed infants.
Sometimes whole families.

The lone, skirted silhouette on a hillside,
bent double with worry and work.

Nowadays, whole villages pitch in,
thanks to satellites and reeking, oil-thirsty machines.

They say it's for the best,
that this is progress. And maybe it is.

Even so, I can't help admiring
your iron persistence. Your horse-sense.

Stone by levered stone, you made a field.
Hand over hand, I reclaim it.

STRUGGLING WITH DESIRE AT SUMMER'S END

The sun a copper ingot above,
    earth boiled dry as an empty kettle below.
    Between the two, a swollen sky that yields nothing.

The gravid grape bursts, uneaten, on the vine.
    Painted face of the flower unfurls mid-air.
    The hummingbird repeatedly tongues its fluted,

lavender throat, seeks sweetened answers.
    But you and I were never nest-builders,
    having passed our apogee, having left the wishbone

blanched and brittle in the threadbare yellow grass.

FEEDING THE DEAD

He is walking toward me, crossing the frost-
ruined lawn under a rainwashed sky.
He's come for overripe tomatoes,
which I'm harvesting by the bagful in the hothouse.

On a day like this, with the light all askew and woodsmoke
perfuming the unsettled air, it's easy to believe he's taken on
flesh once more, that twenty-five pounds of tomatoes
would be enough to save him from nothingness.

That the unadulterated blood of the vine could restore him,
leach the smoke from his lungs.

Smoke sifts down as ash falls on rooftops, thickens the harrowed field.
Ash floats on the river whose waters carry defeated mountains,
swell the valley downstream.

Autumn after autumn, a trembling hand holds a match to the hills,
sets bush and tree aflame, blackens meadow and crop,
spurs the bear to greater appetites, the bird to sudden flight.

It is a cold fire that consumes him, too, and so he comes,
emptied out and invisible as e-fumes, for one last taste of the season,
the gently decaying fruit sweet on his tongue.

TO THE BEAR HUNTER WITH DOGS

perhaps you didn't know that, on the morning before his death,
the bear emerged from the brush at the edge of the pond like a
        dark apparition
that a plumed cadre of goldenrod bowed down to him as he passed
that he glistened sleekly in the plain light of day
that he carried the creamy surfeit of summer on his broad back
that the sight of him took my breath away
so that I could not have run if I had wanted to
that the sunstruck hills bore witness to the moment
the still-verdant tamaracks, too
that the flat eye of the pond was a mirror,
holding us in a brief, unified vision
that the first report from your rifle the next morning slapped the
        entire valley awake
that the second was an affront to all hunters
that the bullets burst through my own heart when he was killed
that for three days afterward the woods echoed with the baying of
        your lost hound
then all went silent
that the silver blood of Ursus dripped from the sky at night
that the earth lapped it up at once
that it seemed to have a thirst for such things
that you could comprehend

A DREAM WORTH DYING FOR

Well liberty should be an obvious one
the simple dream of fruit another
take the apple tree in newborn Providence
almost 100 years before Rhode Island was a state
        long taproot probing a dark vein of earth
performing subterranean miracles on behalf of bark and leaf
            that root earnestly mined the loam for treasure
            struck mineral gold in the discarded body
                    of Roger Williams in 1683 or '84
Williams dreamed the good dream of tolerance while he lived
                the end of conflict
        but the tree knew nothing of wars
            or the fickle ideals of men
it merely continued with its own single-minded purpose
curling silently around the body of Roger Williams
        taking on the shape of femur and spine
the skull of the once radically-minded Roger Williams
        upcycling calcium iron protein
into the crisp red orbs held high above the grave
of the abolitionist Roger Williams
        may he rest in peace
    may we all be repurposed thus

WHITE CHRYSANTHEMUMS

November. The bright fields of the farm
finished for another year.
The hired men chopping corn in the rain.

Working all day in the trough of the mountain,
the soil cold and listless
beneath the gnashing blades of the machines.

The farmer's thoughts turn to moving calves into barns,
equipment into the shop for winter repairs.

The hot weight of ripe tomatoes on the vine
no longer a pressing concern. Nor the muskmelon,
with their fragrant, urgent umbilical wounds.

The quiet months approach swiftly.
He's looking forward to those January afternoons
curled up, cat-like, in his armchair by the stove.

From her silent kitchen in the farmhouse,
his wife surveys the lacerated earth.
Recalls the faces of people she won't see again
until the following summer:

the earnest young workers
who dream of owning land themselves one day;
the wide-eyed customers crossing the road
with their cloth shopping bags,
eager to see what new offerings the day has brought.

She thinks of clay jars filled with gladioli,
brilliant spikes of punch reds, corals, lemon-yellows.
What she imagines the tropics must look like.
She places white chrysanthemums in the window.

COMPANY LEAVING

Snow sifted down all afternoon and the plow trucks
passed by every hour, keeping pace until dusk,
when the sky cleared unexpectedly.
The lights had already come on over the hospital parking lot,
bathing everything in an electric-orange glow.

I watched from the window of Room 121
while he went out to brush off the car.
Tried to remember what it was like
to walk unfettered by oxygen canisters and plastic tubing.

Looking out at the night, I pictured myself there,
leaving for home with him and breathing regular air again,
clear and sharp as starlight.

HUSBAND AND WIFE

Once I understood that it was completely out of my hands,
what was hardest for me about the thought of dying
was leaving him behind, but even that was selfish
because what I really wondered about
was who would take my place.

On one of the rare days when he left my side,
I made a list of the possibilities on hospital stationery.
Later, sitting in a chair by the window, he rejected
every one of my suggestions, and we argued about it
the way any married couple might disagree about
what color to paint the house, or where to go on vacation.

TRANSPLANTATION PROCEDURES

"For transport to the recipient hospital, donor lungs are kept inflated at mid-expiration with 50% oxygen in 2 liters of cold Perfadex."

A phone rings and rings in the night.
Nobody answers at first,
but the someone on the other end does not give up.
Shock waves roll through two small towns,
tangle telephone lines, upend households.

"When the recipient is in the operating room, a peripheral venous line and a radial artery line are inserted while the patient is awake. Anesthesia is then induced and the recipient is intubated. A warming blanket is used to cover the upper thorax and the legs."

Death enters the soft skin beneath the jugular,
misses expertly, by centimeters. Moves behind a pane of sterile plastic
       to wait.
Time runs down the crumpled wall, puddles on bent steel.

"Our incision of choice is the clamshell incision....The saw is positioned in such a way as to cut the sternum obliquely."

A person could die this way, waiting for someone
with the right equipment to come along.
Bring a flashlight and rope, bring fresh air and light.

"The recipient operation is performed with cardiopulmonary bypass available on a standby basis."

The heart must be strong to go on beating after catastrophe.
It must be stubborn and brave, a mule heart with a big kick.
Or else the heart of a swan, with room enough for two.

"The right lung transplantation is accomplished first. The left lung is then excised and the donor lung implanted."

Dig down to the center of ruin and have a look around.
There is junk mail, and stacks of scratched Polaroids,
yards of red and blue ribbon. A yellow flood of memories.
Everything must be carefully preserved for later study in the lab.

*"At the termination of the operation, two chest tubes are placed in each
thoracic cavity, the sternum is reapproximated with #5 wires, and the
patient is reintubated."*

Tight, so tight. All available space has been filled,
the remaining oxygen squeezed out.
Not so much as a spare chromosome could fit in here.

*"In the immediate postoperative period, patients require a 1:1
nurse-patient ratio."*

Distant thud of dragonfly wings. Perhaps another Life Flight
            approaching?
A hand reaches in, bringing pain, but also a ceiling to cap it.
The brackish horizon looms into view.

*"Chronic rejection remains the major late complication of lung
transplantation."*

Test for infection, for bone strength.
Test for compression of the spirit.
Thankfully, the body is a resilient shelter,
a regular phoenix of spackle and blood.

NIGHTJAR

(Coming off the ventilator)

The plain brown bird trolls the listening dark for departing souls,
casting an alias out over the mellow September evening like a net.
Capturing what it can in its black glass throat.

It wakes the young woman, who steps cautiously from the feverish
       tent
of sleep. In the exploded silence, she listens to the chuffing brook,
to the bird as it continues its single-minded search.
Holds her breath in the interludes between entreaties.

By the time she is able to focus, the season has changed.
Snow falls on the wrecked garden of summer, on the red water
       pump
that pours rust and black spiders when primed.

Somehow, she has arrived at the wrong gate.
Snake-headed geese roam the shadows,
trampling the path that might lead her back.
The orange crease in the eastern sky is the sun,
come to knock feathers out of untrustworthy clouds.

NIGHTJAR II

(Waking in the ICU)

I was utterly bewitched by the figure on the lawn.
Female, her face upturned, bathed in rainwater.
Tumult of copper leaves at the hem of her cobalt dress.

I kept hoping for a sign, for movement.
Blink of the eye, flick of basalt.
Impossible to look away, lest I miss it.

I fancied her hovering above saffron-colored grass,
but later discovered I was the one floating,
suspended by pharmaceutical wonders, wings of gauze.

When I fell at her feet, my mouth filled with frozen dirt
and I tasted the oozing ferric heart of the earth.
Had the ground grown up around us?

I longed to ask her,
but she was deaf as a stone.
Nearby, her sisters balanced on a nest of naked branches.

They wore squat, brown leather shoes,
starched white leggings, like the nurses did here in the old days.
As evening came on, they attended to me, so tenderly robotic in
        their movements,
so indifferent to my gently melting edges.

SURFACING

"To have the whole air!
To own, for the moment, nothing."
                    —Jane Cooper, "Starting with a Line from Roethke"

The Storm

That summer, the air grew petulant,
difficult to breathe. Tempest after tempest loomed
on the horizon. The last being the worst.
It hooked me right through the chest,
it took me out and out.
My lungs filled with salty water.

Lifeline

Riptide of disintegrating flesh and blood,
the scope of it breathtaking. Caught in its grip,
I emerged far from the known shore
spitting pieces of my lung into my hands,
sipping air through a plastic rope
as I clung to the sinking raft of my body.

The Transplant

If she was there in the room in some form,
hovering above us or watching from a corner,
I will never know.
If she saw the cleaving of skin and muscle,
the smashed plate of bone swept aside
and the unapologetic blade bearing
down on the gnarled air sacs,
first the right and then the left,
I can only guess.
If she witnessed the short thread of my life
suddenly lengthening, gloved hands suturing her fate to mine,
she gave no sign.

Chrysalis

But later, as I floated in a dark chrysalis of anesthetics,
I felt her presence clearly,
germinating like a surf-washed seed
in the unfamiliar loam of my body.
She spoke my name, just once,
and I've never forgotten it
all these years later:
the sound of her voice spilling from my lips.

Surfacing

This must be how we are born.
We surface, rising up from the spectral depths,
straining to grasp that first lustrous, elusive thought.
But it is the need for breath, urgent and terrible,
that propels us toward the world of light.
When I came into it for the second time,
I believed in nothing but air.

HELPLESSNESS

After Dali

Blurred vision for a week. Thinking I was going blind,
not comprehending it was chemical marvels at work.
The corridors of the hospital a white labyrinth
crawling with bruised shadows.

Gingerly stepping around the Beluga-like form
lying in front of the gift shop.

Back in my room, I closed my eyes,
but couldn't stop seeing past the leaky borders of dreams.

Fallen moons and melted clocks
floated in a blue-black sea.

The bloated hours ticked past my ears.
I kept trying to remember how I ever filled them.

BOSTON IN MARCH

In the courtyard at the hospital,
chartreuse blisters erupt
on the bark of the forsythia
and the winter-stunned Japanese maples blanch,
their nakedness suddenly exposed.

Beside a memorial bench,
an azalea explodes in a spray of pink vigor
and the grass, crushed and anemic,
emerges gradually from beneath tattered bandages
of ashen snow.

For days, a southern breeze works to revive it,
and the day comes when the lawn pulses with green lifeblood.
It beckons to the ambulatory and despairing alike,
and to the young nurses in pastel scrubs
who run things here.

THE HEALER

For months, her determined hands
coaxed the sickness up and out of my lungs
until it came to rest, eventually, in her own—
the same way lightning enters a house
through an open circuit: silent, implacable,
and no telling how it might exit again.

ACCEPTANCE

I watch you prepare dinner,
thin blade of the knife slicing easily
through choice backstraps.

You snip away the glossy sinew,
place the meat in a glass pan to marinate.
Red juice mingling with a medley of spices.

If it's true the cells are capable of memory,
then perhaps the heart is grateful to the marksman
who shatters it with a single shot.

As I am grateful to the steady hand that freed her
from the collapsed housing of muscle and tissue
which imprisoned her without warning.

And to the skilled fingers that wielded the scalpel,
opening my own damaged flesh
to the possibility of a second chance.

Such a bold experiment,
this fusion of blood and dreams
which renders everything tender and new.

RISING

In March the men came and set traps,
warning those of us with dogs away.
I walked the water's edge anyway,
determined after a year of sickness
to see the land in each of its seasons again.

The rain came, then the mud.
By June everything had been washed downstream:
the traps, the beaver family, the geese.
The pond formed a rough brown scab of muck
that buckled and cracked in the early summer heat.

When I returned in September,
white moths hovered over a newborn meadow
where the pond had been,
and a solitary sunflower rose from the middle
of the grass like a small yellow sun.

LABOR DAY, 2009

Holiday traffic strung out along the highway,
separate hearts secured in metal boxes

a single crow flying low, skimming river and field,
ignoring the fully-tasseled corn in favor of carrion

if it hears the distant bleat of a siren it gives no sign,
flaps like a dark thought above the clamor.

Some of it was rumor:

He had been drinking.
He was texting his girlfriend.

Some of it terrible and true:

He crossed the line.
A young woman in the other car.

Most of it mercifully unknowable:

She never knew what hit her.

Two days earlier, she bought flowers at the farmer's market.
Photograph of an infant on her keychain.

When asked, she said that she was raising him on her own.
She said it shyly but proudly. She was a teller at the First National
        bank.

Did she think of the way he gazed up and saw only her,
her eyes a window framing the world for him

The road straight and dry
a terrible accident

20

the crow gliding blackly on
the boy went on growing without her

THE DAY YOU LEFT FOR KUNDUZ

It was snowing and I was reading Ovid,
of the many tales of forbidden love,
the lost honor of youth.

Later the clouds cleared
and a sluggish Hunter's Moon rose,
so weighed down by the world
it refused to carry any more sorrow,
yet I found one more to offer up anyway:
on the whitewashed plain of the field,
a stitching of tracks, fine as a paper chain,
ending in a single white wingprint.

Which wasn't enough of a sacrifice,
it seems, because the next morning,
those ever-wrathful gods burned
a Chinese restaurant to the ground,
threatened a whole block of buildings
with the hot breath of their greed.

Afterward, it looked a lot like the pictures
of the place you were going.
Scorched stone and smoking sky.
The weary faces of the dispossessed.

AUGURY

Together they went up
the rough knuckle of the mountain,
an as-yet un-sundered pair
but somewhere close to the summit,
their path divided.

The signs were star-writ,
there was something in the way their shadows diverged
beneath the moonlight
although they walked side by side.

Cold night entered her then,
poured through the node
where his missing rib fused with hers,
and her heart divided, froze.

That was the treacherous spot where they stopped,
where they turned back.

Stricken,
she followed his boot prints
down the slope through the motionless,
silver-tipped trees.

Back on the floor of the world,
they joined a party
already in progress
in the granite-shod house
where he took his first steps
where he became the kind of man
who bought blazes of blue delphinium for his wife
on a whim.

She walked among the strangers in the familiar room,
already a ghost to them,
her limbs sheathed in ice.
She touched nothing,
spoke to no one.

Later he tried to warm her
revive her with hot coffee and blankets.
The woodstove clucked and glowed with heat.
Finally he curled his body around hers,
but she continued to tremble.
She could not shake that chill.

LOVESICK

The four dogs follow me from one room to the next,
hounding me. They expect their daily walk,
don't understand why I'm lingering indoors
when we could be outside.

I'm reminded of the year I was house-bound,
unable to lace up my own shoes.
How they would burst through the door
after exploring on their own,
smelling of moss and dried leaves,
carrying news of the weather in their fur.

They don't recognize this as another kind of illness,
but it is. A disequilibrium of the heart and mind.
Too much of one, not enough of the other.
Once again, I find myself trapped in a body
that yearns for the impossible.

This thing that seethes and howls within:
if I turned it loose, would it run off into the hills,
sneak back to nibble the lustful edges of my dreams?
I strain against the leash that binds me,
the frayed rope of comfort and trust.

WHAT TREMBLES ON THE SCALES

(Borrowing a line from Anna Akhmatova)

Her whole life, she sensed it:
On one side, the red flowers blooming at dusk.
A gilded flute and violin.
All of the words she strove to master.
On the other, a great black wing descending.
Nothing beyond.
Even the hateful gate is absent.

In the interim,
a familiar angel visits,
aged and bearing mop and pail.
When she beckons, what choice does one have
but to follow?
Frightened but willing.
Ready to do the work required.

REMAINS

Startled into brief flight,
the partridge slid to a stop
on the icy surface of the brook.
The two dogs, ruffled and breathing heavily,
closed in quickly.

Fearing an explosion of blood and feathers,
I tried to turn away.
But it was over in an instant.
One vigorous shake
and the bird crossed effortlessly,
almost gracefully,
over the threshold that separates
known from unknown.

Puzzled, the dogs sniffed at it,
then one picked up the prize,
dropped it at my feet.
I reached down to pick it up,
surprised by what remained:
the still-warm body,
the weight of folded wings.

FAR GONE

The winter folded me into itself, its stiff white peaks,
unyielding cream of cloud, layer upon layer of snow.
The months settled on my shoulders; I wore them
like an oversized shawl, buried myself in temporal lace.
When we fought, I made a veil to cover my eyes,
tried widowhood on for size.

But each afternoon, just before you'd come home,
the sky would begin to lighten, as if by magic.
A blue ribbon pinned to the collapsed horizon of another day.
I'd rise from our bed, begin preparing the evening meal;
a little light and heat would enter the house at last,
the aroma of garlic and oil, curl of spice and fire.

By February, stacks of ice threatened to bring the roof down,
great slabs of solid water suspended above our heads,
and because you said you almost welcomed it—
the laying down of burdens, the change of scenery—
I knew the blackness had spread from me to you,
the way fruit in a barrel rots from the inside out,
no way of knowing until the whole mess
is too far gone to save.

THE CROSSING

June rain rinses the land and the earth exhales,
silver filaments of mist stretching up
from the hills to touch the low-lying clouds,
lake and river brimming,
every green thing swollen with moisture.

I am thinking now of Carrie,
how in March it was much the same,
the rain coming down steadily for days
scouring the snow from the slopes.

The water-addled brook near her house succumbed,
the icy flow surging up over the bridge,
inundating the yard,
much in the same way
that the cancer spread throughout her body:
headlong, belligerent, determined.

She refused chemo, radiation.
Kept on with the reiki treatments,
did Qigong until she could no longer stand on her own.
The nurse continued to come and go daily.

Two days before she died, we drove out to her place.
As we crossed the bridge, the brook lapped
at the running boards of the truck like a frothing, rabid animal.
In the end, we made it through,
parked in the sleet-pocked pond that was her driveway,
with no thought of how we'd make it back again.

ADVANCED BEGINNERS

B. couldn't swim. She grew up in Gloucester,
a village famous for its drowned fishermen.
At summer camp, she could never pass the level of beginner
because she couldn't hold her breath underwater,
or above water, for that matter.

Z. was always excused from class.
She sat on the shore watching us swim,
looking owlish in her large, oval-framed glasses,
her lips pursed and blue
although she hadn't been in the lake.

My own heart and lungs quickened
in those spring-fed waters
where I learned to do the crawl
and perfected my breast-stroke.

The year we all became teenagers,
Z. grew tired of being a spectator,
played goalie for the field hockey team at her school.
The summer after that, our last at Spruce Pond,
she was dead.

"It was just too much," her mother told us.
We didn't know if she meant field hockey or the disease.
We were thirteen and living with cement anchors
sunk deep in our leaky chests.

B. was the oldest in her class.
She dog-paddled in the shallows with the first graders
among the water lilies and cloudy rafts of tadpole
while I secretly dated my swim instructor.
Most nights, after vespers, we swam past the docks
and explored each other in the wet, sprouting darkness.
Sometimes I thought of Z.
Had she had ever kissed a boy?

At the end of that summer, B. was promoted to Advanced Beginner.
It was an honorary title.
Everyone knew she wasn't coming back.
To celebrate her promotion,
B. swam out into water over her head.
I followed.

THOUGHTS ON PIGS AND GOATS

When I was a girl my father kept pigs
in a pen made of plywood and corrugated tin.
Eventually they would escape,
but only after they had grown
to the size of baby bulls.

Then they would trample my mother's garden,
tree my sister and me like cats.
For all their girth, we usually didn't hear them coming
until the last moment.

Not long after, a man in a Chevy pickup would come by.
My father would get his rifle from the bedroom,
slip out the back door without a word.
He could never bear to pull the trigger himself,
could never look the pigs in the eye
in that crucial moment.

He must have felt the same thwarted affection toward us,
his family. For years, we lived under one roof,
avoiding each other, ignoring the blue lights
which sometimes illuminated the dooryard late at night.
We never spoke about the pork we ate
at almost every meal each winter.

I myself have always favored goats.
They produce good milk and cheese
and will eat stubborn weeds.
They can be pets.
If I had a flock, I would let them roam the hills,
shear the rough meadows where they were born.

At dusk I would call to them,
"Come, you blunt angels, you fur dolls,"
and they would move toward me,
brass bells announcing their sure-footed approach.

32

BLOOD SUGAR

When it drops
it drops fast,
like a stone
in a glass
of red wine.
You can hear it fall
clear across the room.

An uncle,
eyes bloodshot, half-
closed, beckons
to the pigtailed girl
from the kitchen.
Honey, come here,
sit on my lap.

These things are known
to run in families,
like slow blindness
and swift rage.
Too-sweet blood.
It binds them,
secretly,
thick as starch.

THRESHOLD

For heifer number 1342, one wrong step was all it took.
She lies in clean sawdust, eyes closed, working to breathe,
her spotted sides flaring and shrinking like bellows.
Every few moments, her eyes roll back in their sockets
and she moans softly, as if for mercy.
After chores, the simple action of a rifle will bring it.
But for now, she is half-blind and unable to stand
in this world or the other, and so trapped between the two.

Late summer light comes in through the boards.
The men appraise her critically, estimate her hanging weight,
discuss the cuts they will make. I drift out of the dank barn,
follow the drainage ditch down to the meadow.
Goldenrod parts the spent grass like a river of saffron.

For some reason I keep thinking back
to what my body felt like under his,
the way it once responded but now no more,
our ardor slowly cooling, drifting further and further out,
like finite galaxies after the Big Bang.
I am standing on the fault line of my own life,
the threshold between what is slipping away
and what is possible in the future.

I do not know what kind of step I have taken, whether wrong or
        right,
whether my legs will hold out beneath me;
and for the moment there is only this careful breath, and the next.
There is milk and blood and shit, the certainty of it,
there is the world that must be fed,
there is sawdust to be changed,
fuel to be dispensed into machines and bills to be paid.
That much is solid at least.

Even as the woodcock flies up to the dewy, rising moon,
and the thrush sweetly calls from the edge of the wood,
even as the earth tilts one day closer to its azimuth
and the milkweed swells to its eruptive conclusion,
there is the knowledge that no matter how hard we resist,
the smart crack of a rifle will echo out across a silent field,
and the pickers will pause in their work and look up, and know,
and inevitably bend their heads to the harvest once more.

SPIRITUAL WORKERS IN A PHYSICAL WORLD

It's true that I wanted to run,
but to you, not away,

not from the work.
I knew it would be hard,

this union of cloud and dirt,
frail sun and barbed wire.

You pulled me up through dappled moss,
I held you fast to the earth.

But what anchors you now?
What keeps me from sinking

through the hardpan of your disappointment,
apart from a sturdy pair of boots?

DREAMING IN COLOR

"In Sleep we lie all naked and alone, in Sleep we are united at the heart of night and darkness, and we are strange and beautiful asleep; for we are dying the darkness and we know no death."
—Thomas Wolfe

I.

Earliest summer and the ditch gardens are in full blossom,
pale clumps of wild carrot and campion like forgotten snow
among the conical forests of lupine,
lime-green vines of morning glory twisting and twining,
sending up white flags for miles and miles.

2.

A woman dreamt that a policeman put a golden serpent
in her bed, a coiled letter between bone-colored sheets.
She woke instantly, alone, the house powerless and silent
in the wake of a storm. Outside in the thick darkness,
a single siren trembled like a wavering heart.

3.

Another time, in another town, she was selecting an outfit,
a dress to meet her lover in. Since it was only their second date,
she chose everything with extreme care:
the color of her camisole (black), the wine (white),
even her words. She had expanded her vocabulary
to make room for the overflow of conversation.
While walking back to their cars, she spotted the bright red fruit
that birds refused to eat. He supplied her, at long last,
with the name and the reason: snakeberry.

4.

In the dream, the house seemed real enough.
Solid gray clapboard, green trim, and out front,
the rigid red cedars standing watch over rectangular herb gardens,
sylvan wildflowers cautiously advancing from the shade.
Nobody home, but all was flourishing, including the snake,
spear-headed, stretched full-length across the granite step
like a line carved in stone: here and no further.

SEPARATION

Now there are no appointments to keep,
no deadlines to make. I wake when I'm rested;
if I choose not to make breakfast,
I feel light and hungry all morning.

I answer only to the dogs and their appetites.
They are utterly dependent on me for meals and walks,
affection. If I move from one room to another,
they track my movements with wary eyes.

Apart from their needs, my time is my own.
Nobody minds if the laundry remains unfolded
at the foot of the bed, if dust collects in corners.
Mail gathers in the box at the end of the driveway;
when I think to, I walk out to retrieve it.
Take what I want and leave the rest.

My tracks, and those of the dogs, are the only sign
that someone still lives on this hillside.
Even those are erased by the snow that falls nearly every day.
Sometimes it comes down fast, slanting in from the west
so it looks as though the house is leaning into it,
bearing up under the onslaught of winter.

Two nights ago, after a storm,
a Wolf Moon rose late in the eastern sky.
Sulfur-blue light blazed through the hemlocks
and pooled in the yard. I turned off my lamp
and continued to read in its cool glow.

Each night since then, the moon has grown smaller.
Somewhere I heard that it is pulling away from earth,
venturing further into space year by year,
a wayward satellite.

Meanwhile, inertia holds me in place.
The gravity of indecision.
But there are days, oh, there are days
when I long to be knocked out of this lonely orbit,
carried off by a rousing cosmic tide.

MY DRESS STILL HANGS THERE

After Frida Kahlo

Before I had even moved out, she began moving in,
her clothes hanging beside mine in the closet.
My little black dress, the only one I owned,
side by side with her lace-lined red teddy
on its satiny, child-sized hanger.

The pictures of us came down off the wall,
replaced by a glitter-spackled 8X10 of her
on the kitchen counter, front and center,
tight little tummy and pierced belly button exposed.

I learned plenty of other things about her, too,
while I was there:
she read romance novels,
kept candied vodka in the freezer.
She wore the same size shoe as me.

I drank the vodka, straight out of the bottle,
while I packed.
Resisted the urge to smash her photo,
piss in every corner of the house
like an ousted vixen.
I left that dress hanging there like a shed skin.

CONNECTED

Think of it: each strand of silk in an ear of corn
is attached to a single grain of pollen at one end,
an ovarian kernel on the other.

Imagine the dank potential in a square acre of earth,
in a swaying, cubic foot of air.
All those perfect golden squares.

Now envision the ways we are connected:
children, memories, a mountain.
You on your side, me on mine.

Still sharing a view of that blanched peak
When you sigh and turn over in your sleep,
the wind sobs outside my window.

Strands of my hair dangle like last year's witch hazel
from the cobwebbed eave above your head.
They weave their way into my dreams.

SUSPENSION

When I could no longer bear to think of him
in that distant northern village,
or the impossible length and breadth of a year,
of all that needed to be accomplished between
its frozen beginning and end:
twelve months of dust settling on letters that remained sealed,
the dog's face seeming to age in silver double-time,
children growing inch by painful inch.

When I grew weary of straining slow hours
through rough cheesecloth,
I thought instead of the crab apple blossoming on the lonely hill,
of bees making noisy love to the misshapen russet globes
in the shaggy grass at its base.

Recalled the flensing downpours of November
giving way to the first soundless snow
and how the denuded rose bush endured beside the cellar hole
in the woods, its thorns bristling like icy quills
beneath a ceiling of cold light.

That's when I felt my own bones settle down to wait
like a shuttered summer house,
to see what would happen in the hushed lacuna
between this new life and the old.

X AND Y

Suppose what he wanted was
a skinny girlfriend,
a girl with fine hair,
bare below the hips,
no hips, no swing,
no rhythm, not yet
but one day her spring-loaded,
elliptical belly which will bear
the high-water mark of their desire
like a mixed message of pride
and regret
(for the rest of her life)
she will covet
smooth skin, fine hair, skinny hips,
but in exchange she will acquire rhythm,
the rings of her heart
contracting and expanding
with seasons of want and plenty,
the flux of attraction and repulsion
a tide within her,
ruled by an irresistible domestic moon
she does not yet understand,
it is a horizon she cannot yet see beyond.

MENSTRUAL POEMS

"Blood is family—always"
—Caroline Myss, co-author, *The Creation of Health*

I.

Dear lost child,
I want to tell you
about the different kinds of blood
that bind us,
strong as a garland
woven from garlic
and blue cohosh.
Stronger, even,
than death.

To fill you in on
what you believe you've missed:
a scarlet torrent sluicing
over a dam made of bone,
funneling down to a whirlpool
of clotted grief.
Like cold pudding
stuck to the bottom
of a pan.

That's all.
You, being the clot,
would have discovered self-ablution in time.
Given the chance,
you, too, would have become adept
at scrubbing with steel wool.

2.

Dear Mother,
I've never told you of
those late, late hours,
my throat spouting heat
and guilt into the room,
too awful to swallow.
Painting the floor crimson with it,
the cat watching from the bed.

How, in the morning,
all sins licked away,
the cat, full-bellied,
sated,
told with a lionish smile
how it tasted
like the bitter floor
of your womb.

3.

Dear Grandmother,
forty days of this and
your carafe of cut-crystal
runneth over! Make use of it,
you would have said.

A dye for linens, then,
ochre sheets and tablecloths
for every occasion.

4.

Oh, my little iron-willed Mother,
I want you to know
I am more than
cranberry-colored tubes
sandwiched between hospital walls
like a coded tragedy.

I am a red ampersand,
frying pan between my teeth,
hot brick in my fist.
I've come to it late,
but you'll be glad to know
I've finally learned how to cook.

ON LEARNING MY EX-HUSBAND IS GOING TO BE A FATHER

It was a secret the two of them carried for months,
like a scarlet bird of paradise nesting in ferric New England soil.
I could not have been more surprised to stumble upon it.

I immediately thought back to that double pink line in the bathroom,
how it seemed to blur and bleed at the edges of the white, tiled
        field,
how in the mirror over my shoulder I could see his upper lip
        trembling.

And then it was gone,
dissolving as swiftly and miraculously as it had appeared.
It became a gravid secret that we kept between us for years.

But soon there will be something much more substantial
than a winged ghost between them.
Moment by moment it is unfolding, taking on weight and form.

Oh, how it presses on me, tender as a pinched nerve.

BY WAY OF APOLOGY

That first morning I was up absurdly early after a late flight.
My first thought was of you, sleeping warm in our bed across the
        Atlantic
as gusts of fine rain misted the shops and homes of Dingle and,
in a steeply sloping pasture above town,
the sturdy, dappled backs of horses as they chomped wet grass.

A man in a brown cap stood at the wooden gate, holding a pair of
        halters.
He was smoking a pipe and the sweet, rich scent hung in the
        motionless air.
He gazed at the horses, making no move toward them,
paying no attention to me as I passed by.
The rain had soaked his jacket thoroughly.

In that moment, I wished you were there, seeing it with me,
the man and the horses, the bright grass and dark sea.
But then I heard your voice in my head,
saying it was too much like someone's *idea* of Ireland.
The wildly blooming walls of fuchsia,
clipped sheep roaming narrow streets
and seals popping in and out of swells, selkie-like,
at the base of cliffs.

The flare of anger I felt toward you then was like a soft volcano
rumbling up from the center of my seething core.
Looking back, I can name it for what it was:
envy in its simplest form. For which I apologize.

I begrudged that Irish farmer his contentment,
his surety of place. As I coveted yours,
in your oak-and-granite corner of the world.
You let me go, as easily as one drops the reins,
let me discover for myself what you'd always suspected:
that the grass is no greener on the other side.
Not even in Ireland.

READING MILOSZ IN THE EXAM ROOM

she flew like a homing pigeon
straight through the floor-to-ceiling window
into a sky the color of used dishwater

banking around the Prudential like a plane
then out over clam-shaped Massachusetts Bay
swinging north along the coastal route
beating the Amtrak home by an hour
or that's how it went in her head anyway

waiting alone for twenty minutes now
she's been dreading
the faux-oak door opening
keeps thinking she hears voices just beyond it
the doctor and nurse conferring
she tries to listen
to not listen at the same time

will it be bad news
will they order more tests
they always want more tests
will she have to spend the night
she had not thought to pack a bag

the bottoms of her feet itch
she is wearing a long black skirt
just last month
it was two sizes too big
now it's even looser in the waist
what if it's rejection
aspergillus lymphoma
so many things could go wrong

she's reading Milosz
or trying to read
she glances down at the page
the words clutch at her heart
which flails wildly against her ribs like a caged monkey

each time she comes to the city
this is precisely how she feels
disconnected from the rise and fall of tides
the shadows of clouds moving over the hills
dispossessed of the life she is trying to build for herself

just then she hears the click of the handle turning
closes the book on her lap
it is heavy and solemn
something solid to brace against
as the bowed shape of the future
glides into the examination room

WRITING AS THERAPY

Subconscious

Every time I try to write, you come to mind.
I haven't seen you in months.
Yet I close my eyes and there you are, big as a mountain.
Casting your shadow all over my new page.

Bridge

Here's where I want to be: hip-deep in the stream of my life.
Here's where I am: snarled in the shallows like flotsam.
What I need is a bridge that spans the middle distance.
Or a pair of waders.

Young Bride

What I remember most about that day:
Stack of nickel-gray clouds unexpectedly parting.
Other last-minute miracles:
Windswept carpet of crabapple blossoms underfoot.
The cooing of doves just before midnight.
Calling *I do. I do. I do.*

No-fault

This phrase feels untrue. Surely I am to blame.
Otherwise you wouldn't enter my thoughts any time you please.
Nor would the extravagant white gown, which in the end I did not
        choose.
So many regrets.

Graft

For a long time, I was in disbelief.
As if I had cut off my own hand.
I kept waiting for it to grow back.
To grow into the life I had reshaped for myself.
Instead, I grew around the gnarled stump of the old one.

Writing as Therapy

In the meantime, I keep working at it.
This is as safe a place to put it all down as any.
Everyone writes, but hardly anybody reads poetry anymore.

SOJOURN

Low-Density Residential

I am trying to accept this place
for what it is,
with its screeching toddlers
and indiscriminate,
nighttime artillery drills
by the homegrown militia.

I balance this with the mosaic
of sun-glossed oak leaves
outside my bedroom window,
with the mergansers that nested
on the shores of the shallow lake
this summer.

Sojourn

Bay-side that first morning,
I woke and kissed salt-air,
celebrated the absence of sound
with champagne and juice,
mused over the spiny pink flowers
tumbling over the garden gate
for close to an hour.
How good it felt to get away.

Neighbors

I hear the chuffling cough of the Sheltie
that lives on the corner of Victoria and Greenfield,
and, moments later, the echoing boom
of the Mastiff-mix from behind the red
stockade fence next door. I learned their names
long before I learned those of their owners.

With time, I mastered the names
given to the soil as well:
Buxton silt loam, Hollis-complex.
Hosta and astilbe grow well here.
In the backyard, lamia spreads
like a silver pool,
conceals the crumbling foundation of the house.

I make a border of tulips and narcissi,
hopeful that next spring,
some other couple will be living here
to see them come up.

Early July

How far away the grass-thatched dunes
and salmon-colored bluffs of the Cape seem.
The sea is a closed blue door I stumble toward,
cloud-blind but determined.

EXPATS

Never mind Eve's trusting heart,
or Adam's wet, pliant rib
from which it was fashioned.

It was the verse that contained the tree
on which the word blossomed
and became the fruit.

The same tree that bears the adulterated weight
of the limbed snake for an eternity.
Bark buckling under the load.

Stunted, it continues to grow,
roots spreading from that first,
ruined garden even now.

Taking on new material,
a new form as it spreads.
Trying out a new tongue.

Still, we recognize the shape,
flimsy green ladder
angled optimistically heavenward.

THE LAST GARDEN

The party over, I exchange this choker of black pearls
for a red flannel nightgown. Dig my bed with fork and spoon,
pull an afghan of taupe grass and sienna-colored leaves
up to my shoulders. Pillow of thyme for my head.
A golden nub of cornstalk presses into my hip.
I lie this way for hours, half-asleep,
jaundiced face of the moon floating above me.

Tarnished fruit hangs like shriveled paper lanterns from the pear
        tree,
and the last of the tart, yellow apples drops with a thump into the
        ditch.
From a dark corner, a tenacious heap of rusted brassicas heckles me.
I stuff my ears with straw, but they raise their voices higher.
This could go on for a long time.

Just before dawn, frost dazzles the world with silver light.
Fatally astonished, the plants fall silent at last.
I slip back under my stiff covers,
let the sink full of dishes go unwashed until spring.

WINTER NIGHT, THINKING OF THE FARM

Sitting by the woodstove eating glazed pears from a jar
I suddenly remember how, one morning during a long dry spell
     years ago,
the dawn sky jettisoned a thick, glossy white wedge of cloud.

Remember how it drifted down like an immense, pearly sponge,
as if it wished to sop up the brown trickle of river water
that lay pooled in the valley below.

How it left the latticework of crops ravished with dew
when the sun burned through midday,
every leaf and fruit lavishly drenched.

Later the old Ford chugged through steaming fields,
laden with ripe corn and the half-grown men who had picked it,
juice from ripe melons running down their newly stubbled chins.

Most of them have scattered to the winds by now,
some have children, careers in the city.
Two done in by their own hand.

I think of them as they were then, young and full of dreams,
finding pleasure in the simple things,
like eating last year's canned pears by the fire.

GRAFTING AS METAPHOR

One spring at the farm
a year after my transplant
we grafted 200 tomato seedlings—
Maxifort rootstock to scions of Beefsteak
and Heirloom varieties.

Three of us worked at a long bench
in the manufactured warmth of the greenhouse
while a blizzard swirled outside,
a hackneyed April Fool's joke.

Splicing the plants together was like surgery,
monotonous and delicate at the same time.
You had to slit the fragile, celadon stem tissue
with a double-edged razor,
then attach the cutting at a precise angle,
bind the oozing, wounded juncture with tiny clips.

It was impossible to guess which ones would take,
which would fail.
The successful unions formed
a seamless bond, put down roots,
flourished in the field.

ROULETTTE

1.

the horses cross the minefield
beneath a punishing sun

because he is a poet
each step wounds him terribly

because he is a soldier
he does not turn his head

he knows there are things worse
than what's buried beneath the blowing sand

he puts his ear to the dry earth
but the desert maintains its ancient silence

2.

because of the women softly singing
in the rain in the dark,
the television stays on all night

because of the nail-bitten army,
because of the official needle in the obedient arm,
the olanzapine, the benzodiazepine

because there are two angels standing by,
one from above and one from below,
the whiskey

because of the complicated marriage
of oil and spangled water,
the single bullet in the hollow chamber.

NOTE TO SELF ON THE SIXTH ANNIVERSARY
OF MY LUNG TRANSPLANT

It's not as if you wanted her to die so that you could go on living.
You just had this narrow ledge of hope that you walked on tiptoe,
putting one foot in front of the other.
Not daring to look up or down.

She might have been anyone, then.
A mom, an attorney,
a high school dropout.
Endless possibilities.
Like God, she was faceless, ageless.
Strange to think that you breathe as one now.

Back then, you were still an unknown yourself,
trying to decide whether or not to buy boots,
if you'd be around next winter to wear them.

Oddly, you think of her heart sometimes,
that severed, nuanced pump,
beating on in someone else's chest now.
Does it desire the same things that she once loved:
men of a certain size and shape, for instance,
or salsa and pistachio ice cream?

And sometimes, when you look in the mirror
and your right pupil is radically dilated,
you wonder if the doctors are wrong,
that it's not a side effect of the medications
so much as it's her,
come to the window of your shared body for a look around.

It's been six years since the clot she unknowingly carried
detonated like a bomb at the base of her skull,
washing her brain clean as a blackboard,
the walls of her spirit imploding in on themselves.

And what about you?
Could it be that you are an amalgam,
the scarred intersection where two lives collided?
The letter you keep folded in your bureau drawer,
the one that begins, "We wanted to tell you about our daughter...."
still leaves you guessing.

THE NEGOTIATOR

That cough, wet and full-sounding,
like a thrown mop,
is pulled from a deep pocket
just below your heart.
It has me up nights.

When your chest quiets,
other worries swarm:
how to keep the locks unpicked,
the student loans paid,
what to do about the cat in the window
of the abandoned house down the road.

When I was a girl,
it was the Soviets
who colored my dreams
mushroom gray.
I'd wake, sweating,
negotiating with God:

keep the bombs from falling,
keep the sour peace between
my parents from curdling,
and I swear I'll never lie again,
I'll do long division until
my mind fractures into pieces.

Now I broker similar deals
on your behalf, your back to mine,
the slow rise and fall of your breathing,
the one-sided conversation
I hold with the wall,
listening my way through the night.

HAPPY WOMEN

don't fall in love often
eat what they like
wear their hair like a garden
overcome with wildness

they hop buses to distant coasts
find their way in the night
swallow the moon like a fat white pill

happy women walk city streets heeled and proud
toe the muddy bottom of riverbeds
dive deep to find the weighted stones

when happy women love
they throw the gate open
hold back a fistful each of green apples
and yellow-striped snakes

A QUESTION REMAINS

Sometimes the sun shining through a pine seems familiar,
needles spinning the rays into a cat's eye
of tinseled light on the lawn.
In those moments I can almost remember
the other life I traded for this new one,
the smell of that country, water and pitch,
hot granite and cool earth.

In that earlier incarnation I was somebody's wife,
beloved, sheltered, some even said the better half,
but still desperate to feel the rolled 'r's and smooth 'l's
of another language on my tongue,
to know the names of stars
and the reason why the moon, flushed and swollen,
seemed to hover like an anxious lover on certain nights.

And I still have no explanation for why,
the summer after I left,
one of the paired apple trees that we planted that first year
suddenly shed its leaves and dropped its fruit,
as if shocked by something the wind had said.
That winter the branches fell, one by one,
lay in the deep snow like amputated limbs.

Mice and fungus went to work,
and finally, out of pity,
my father brought his chainsaw in the spring,
severed the dead heartwood from its roots.

ABOUT THE AUTHOR

Nylah Lyman's poems have previously appeared in *Bellevue Literary Review, Cider Press Review, Hunger Mountain*, and *Poetry Quarterly*, as well as other journals. She holds an MFA in Creative Writing from the University of Southern Maine's Stonecoast program, and has taught workshops focusing on healing through poetry. In 2016, she was selected to attend a writing residency at La Muse in Labastide-Esparbairenque, France. She enjoys traveling and learning new languages, and is an enthusiastic equestrian. She resides in Cape Elizabeth, Maine, with the novelist Kevin St. Jarre and their menagerie of rescued animals.

ACKNOWLEDGMENTS

Grateful acknowledgement is made to the editors of the publications
where some of the poems in this collection
first appeared.

Arcadia Magazine (now Emerald City): "Dreaming in Color"

Bellevue Literary Review: "The Healer"

Big River Poetry Review: "Boston in March"

Cider Press Review: "Threshold"

Coe Review: "Sojourn"

Common Ground Review: "The Negotiator"

Hunger Mountain: "Connected"

The Lindenwood Review: "Thoughts on Pigs and Goats"

Poetry Quarterly: "On Learning My Ex-Husband Is Going to be a
Father"

Red Ochre LiT: "Feeding the Dead"

The Sow's Ear Poetry Review: "Happy Women"

"Making a Field" was chosen by the Poetry Barn to be included
as part of an ekphrastic project hosted by the Arts Society of
Kingston, New York.